5/07

D0578256

In 1956, the police caught a bomber. He had been terrorizing New York City for 16 years.

TRUE or FALSE?

The New York Times

© 1957, by The New York Times Company.

as Second-Class Matter,
Office, New York.

NEW YORK, TUESDAY, JANUARY 22, 1957.

Times Square, New York 36, N.
Telephone LAckawan

SUSPECT IS HELD AS 'MAD BOMBER'; HE ADMITS ROLE

Files of Ediso C Lead to Ex-Employe n Waterbury —Extradition Is Planned

NO EVIDENCE IN HOME

Worker Quoted as Saying He Was 'Gassed' at Plant, Contracted Tuberculosis

The police here announced rly today that a 54-year-old an had admitted that he is the called Mad Bomber. The po- said the man had confessed aterbury, Conn., where he is questio

M

Text

ANK.
The fou
the 1
today t
Eisenho
Middle
In a
their m
istan
the Eis
design
the Mi
the ec
people.
The

Before anyone knew who the bomber was, a criminal profiler had figured out what he would be wearing when he was arrested!

EVIDENCE EVIDENCE EVIDENCE EVIDENCE EVIDENCE EVIDENCE EVIDENCE

TRUE!

A criminal profiler studied the details of this case. He decided the Mad Bomber was a middle-aged European man. He lived in Connecticut. AND he wore a suit with a double-breasted jacket. (That's a jacket with two rows of buttons.)

Meet George Metesky, the Mad Bomber, who lived in Waterbury, Connecticut. Note the double-breasted suit underneath his overcoat.

Metesky's profiler was Dr. James Brussel. Brussel got Metesky exactly right. In the process, he made criminal profiling famous. Keep reading to find out more about criminal profiling.

Book design Red Herring Design/NYC

Library of Congress Cataloging-in-Publication Data
Beres, D. B. 5-14-07
Killer at large : criminal profilers and the cases they solve! / by D.B. Beres.
p. cm. — (24/7 : science behind the scenes)
Includes bibliographical references and index.
ISBN-13: 978-0-531-12065-1 (lib. bdg.)   978-0-531-17526-2 (pbk.)
ISBN-10: 0-531-12065-1 (lib. bdg.)   0-531-17526-X (pbk.)
1. Criminal profilers. 2. Criminal investigation. I. Title.
HV6080.B434 2007
363.25—dc22   2006020869

1 2 3 4 5 6 7 8 9 10 R 16 15 14 13 12 11 10 09 08 07

KILLER AT LARGE

Criminal Profilers and the Cases They Solve!

D.B. Beres

WARNING: All of the cases in this book are true. They involve bombings, murder—and cheating in school.

Franklin Watts®
A Division of Scholastic Inc.
New York • Toronto • London • Auckland • Sydney
Mexico City • New Delhi • Hong Kong
Danbury, Connecticut

CONTENTS

FORENSIC 411

Here's the 411 on what criminal profilers really do.

These cases are 100% real. Find out how criminal profilers helped solve these mysteries.

15 Case #1:
The Case of the Mad Bomber

A series of bombings terrorizes New York City and baffles the police. Can a criminal profiler help find the bomber?

A serial bomber is nabbed in New York City.

27 Case #2:
The Case of the Too-Hot Fire

Firefighters discover a body inside a burning house, and a profiler takes the case.

Investigators are called after a suspicious fire in Florida.

35 Case #3:
The Case of the Mysterious Hacker

A university's computer network is under attack. Can a cyber-profiler find the hacker?

A computer profiler tracks a hacker in Montreal, Quebec.

FORENSIC DOWNLOAD

Here's your guide to the past, present, and future of criminal profiling.

YELLOW PAGES

What happens when a crime is committed and there isn't much evidence? How do police begin to find a suspect?

FORENSIC 411

Anyone could have done it, right? *Wrong.* Criminal profilers can help narrow down the search. Before you get too psyched and jump ahead, read this section.

IN THIS SECTION:

▶ how CRIMINAL PROFILERS really talk;

▶ what kind of PEOPLE they are;

▶ who else is working the CRIME SCENE.

In Your Head

Criminal profilers have their own way of speaking. Find out what their vocabulary means.

suspect
(SUHS-pekt) someone thought to be responsible for a crime

"This doesn't look like an accident. I'd say we've got ourselves a homicide."

psychology
(sye-KOL-uh-gee) the scientific study of the human mind and human behavior

homicide
(HOM-uh-side) a murder

"Psycho" has to do with the mind.

"Ology" means "the study of."

"Profilers aren't magicians. They just know their psychology. They can tell us a lot about our suspect."

criminology
(KRIM-un-OL-uh-gee) the scientific study of crime, criminals, and criminal behavior. An expert in criminology is called a *criminologist*.

"We need an expert in criminology for this case, because the facts don't make sense."

JANE DOE
SUPERVISORY SPECIAL AGENT

"See if you can get someone in criminal profiling down here to the crime scene."

criminal profiling
(KRIM-uh-nul PRO-file-ing) the use of crime scene evidence and psychology to predict a criminal's personality and habits

Say What?

Here's some other lingo a profiler might use on the job.

"At first glance, this looks like a random crime. But I want to see if there was a motive here."

motive
(MOH-tiv) a reason for doing something

MO
(EM-oh) a term for how a criminal operates. It's short for *modus operandi*. That's Latin for "method of operation." *"The guy has the same **MO** every time he robs a bank."*

perp
(purp) a person who has committed a crime. It's short for *perpetrator*. *"Don't worry. We're going to catch this **perp** and put him in jail."*

"I want to know what his behavior means."

stats
(stats) official numbers about events that have happened in the past. It's short for *statistics*. *"According to the **stats**, the number of violent crimes has decreased since 1994."*

behavior
(bih-HAYV-yer) the way a person acts or responds to certain conditions. Behavioral sciences are sciences that study the way people behave.

9

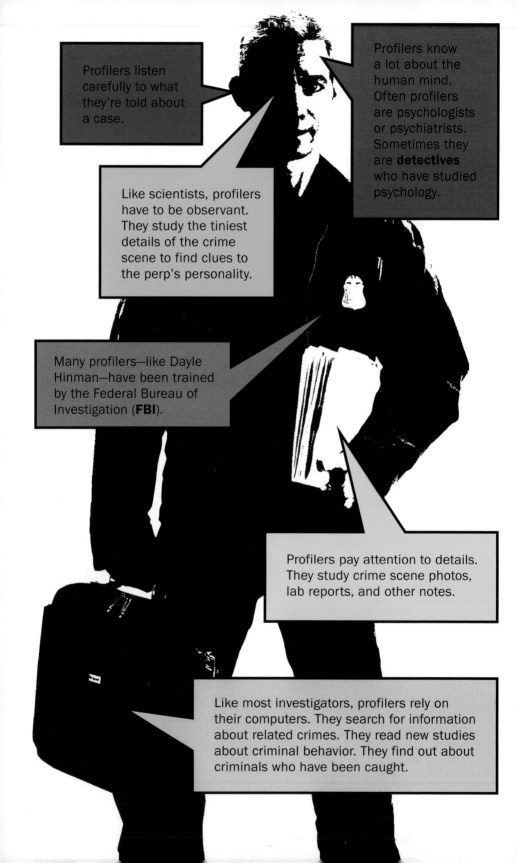

Profile of a Profiler

What do profilers do, and how do they do it?

Most criminals don't drop **ID** cards at the scene of a crime. Many don't leave fingerprints or **DNA evidence**. But to a good profiler, everything a criminal does is evidence.

Profilers look at the details of a crime. From those details they try to describe the criminal. "Profilers narrow the field of suspects," says Dayle Hinman. She has done profiling work for 26 years.

Are police looking for a man or a woman? Is their suspect angry, or cool and calculating?

Steps to Creating a Profile

▶ Profilers' first step is to gather information. Profilers look at crime scene photos. They study all details of the crime. They get to know the victim.

▶ Next, they look at statistics about solved crimes. They ask what type of person has done this kind of crime in the past. Bombers, for instance, tend to be men. Poisoners tend to be women.

▶ The profiler then pulls the information together to create a profile of the criminal.

What kind of person makes a good profiler? Take a look at the profile on the left.

The Forensic Team

Criminal profilers work as part of a team. Here's a look at some of the experts who help solve crimes.

FORENSIC DNA SPECIALISTS

They collect DNA from traces of body fluids, hair, or skin left at the scene. Then they use this evidence to identify victims and suspects.

CRIMINAL PROFILERS

They study the details of a crime and create a profile, or description, of the criminal.

DETECTIVES OR AGENTS

They direct the crime investigation. They collect information about the crime, interview witnesses, identify suspects—and arrest them if there's enough evidence!

TRACE EVIDENCE SPECIALISTS

They collect trace evidence at the scene. That includes fibers, tire tracks, shoe prints, and more. Can this evidence lead them to a criminal?

MEDICAL EXAMINERS

They're medical doctors who investigate suspicious deaths. They try to find out when and how someone died. They often direct other members of the team.

TRUE-LIFE
CASE FILES!

24 hours a day, 7 days a week, 365 days a year, criminal profilers are solving mysteries.

IN THIS SECTION:

▶ how a MAD BOMBER was caught 16 years after he planted his first bomb;

▶ how a PROFILER led police to an arsonist and murderer;

▶ how a profiler discovered A PLOT to steal military secrets over the Internet!

Here's how criminal profilers get the job done.

What does it take to solve a crime? Good profilers don't just make guesses. They're like scientists. They follow a step-by-step process.

As you read the case studies, you can follow along with them. Keep an eye out for the icons below. They'll clue you in to each step along the way.

 At the beginning of each case, the profilers identify **one or two main questions** they need to answer.

 Their next step is to **gather and analyze evidence.** Profilers collect as much information as they can. They study it to figure out what it means.

 Along the way, profilers come up with theories to explain what happened. They test these theories against the evidence. Does the evidence back up the theory? **If so, they've reached a conclusion.**

The Case of the Mad Bomber

A series of bombings terrorizes
New York City and baffles the police.
Can a criminal profiler help
find the bomber?

The Bomber Is Back

A bomb explodes in a New York City theater, and police are stumped.

It was December 2, 1956. There were only three weeks until Christmas. Holiday shoppers bustled along the streets of Brooklyn. Then, at 7:55 P.M., a loud blast shook the ground. Smoke poured out of the Paramount movie theater. A crowd ran out in panic.

The Mad Bomber had struck again!

Everyone in New York knew about the bomber. He'd been planting bombs in the city for 16 years. No one had been killed. But the Paramount bombing injured six people.

Each of the Mad Bomber's **devices** was more powerful than the last. It seemed only a matter of time before someone was killed.

Yet police still had no real clues to the bomber's identity. They knew he had some technical training. His bombs were complex and hard to build. They even had notes from the

The Paramount movie theater in Brooklyn, New York. This photo was taken in 1956. On December 2, a bomb exploded inside the theater. It had been placed by the Mad Bomber.

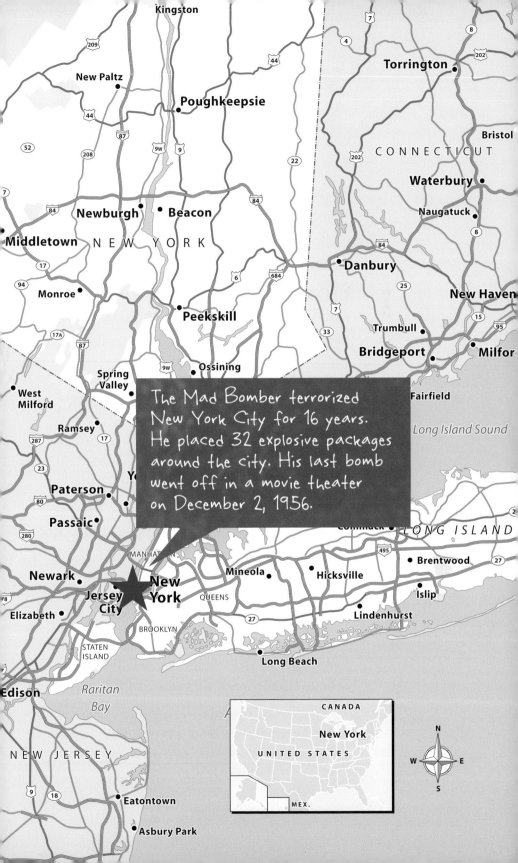

The Mad Bomber terrorized New York City for 16 years. He placed 32 explosive packages around the city. His last bomb went off in a movie theater on December 2, 1956.

bomber. Each time he struck, he left a letter written in block letters. He signed each letter, "F.P."

But after 16 years, they had no idea where to look for "F.P." They were desperate. An inspector in the New York City crime lab decided to try something new. He paid a visit to a criminal psychiatrist named Dr. James Brussel.

Psychiatrist or Detective?

Can a psychiatrist look into the mind of the bomber?

In 1956, criminal profilers were almost unheard of. But Dr. James Brussel had studied criminal behavior for years. He had read about the Mad Bomber. Like everyone else in New York City, he had wondered who the person might be. But when the inspector called, Brussel was surprised. He didn't think he could add much to the case.

Still, Brussel agreed to try. The inspector handed over the bomber's case file. Dr. Brussel opened the file and began studying the Mad Bomber.

Dr. Brussel asked himself, How did the bomber behave? And what did that behavior say about the kind of person he is?

THE QUESTION **?**

Dr. James Brussel was brought in to help solve the Mad Bomber case. He is holding his book *Casebook of a Criminal Psychiatrist*. In it, he talks about his role in the case.

HOW + WHY = WHO

To a profiler, criminals reveal who they are by what they do.

Profilers look at a criminal's behavior in order to get a picture of the person. Here's how it's often done.

1. Staging: What exactly happened at a crime scene? Did the criminal arrange anything deliberately?

2. MO: How does the criminal perform the crimes? What are the patterns to his behavior? Is he calm and careful? Or does he act on impulse?

3. Motive: Why is the criminal committing the crime?

Was it revenge? Anger? To make money?

4. Signature Behaviors: What does this criminal do that seems to be particularly important to him?

5. Victimology: If there are victims of the crimes, who are they? Why would the criminal target these particular people?

Sixteen Years of Terror

Dr. Brussel learns the Mad Bomber's history.

The Mad Bomber planted his first bomb on November 16, 1940. He left it on a window sill at the Consolidated Edison building in New York. Con Edison supplies energy for New York City.

The bomb never exploded. Detectives found a note on the device. It read, "Con Edison crooks, this is for you." Detectives were confused. If the bomb had exploded, the note would have been destroyed. Did the builder purposely make the bomb a dud?

Police found no fingerprints or clues at Con Edison. After a while, no one thought much about it. Then, several months later, the bomber struck again. He left a new device a few blocks from another Con Edison office. This one was wrapped in an old sock. It didn't explode either.

Three months later, the U.S. joined World War II (1939–1945). The bomber sent a letter to the police. The words were cut from

This is a Con Ed plant in the New York area. The Mad Bomber seemed to be angry with this energy company.

The Mad Bomber planted two bombs in Radio City Music Hall. At the time, it was one of the largest indoor theaters in the world. Two people were injured in an explosion there in 1954.

newspapers and pasted onto the page. "I will make no more bomb units for the duration of the war," it read. When the war was over, the bombings would start again, he warned. Con Edison must pay for their "**dastardly** deeds."

For the next nine years, no bombs were found. But the bomber kept sending letters. All the notes were signed, "F.P."

On March 29, 1950, an unexploded bomb turned up in New York's Grand Central Terminal. It was similar to the earlier bombs but more powerful and complex.

Another of the bomber's targets was New York's Grand Central Terminal. The bomber placed a total of five bombs in this railroad station.

Then a bomb exploded in a phone booth at the New York Public Library. Another exploded at Grand Central Terminal. Over the next six years, the Mad Bomber planted dozens of bombs. Finally, the Paramount Theater bombing led police to Dr. Brussel.

Creating the Profile

After studying the bomber's crimes, Dr. Brussel created a surprisingly specific profile.

Dr. Brussel carefully studied the evidence in the Mad Bomber's case file. He also used his own knowledge of criminal behavior. Then he developed theories about the evidence.

Theory: The bomber was male.
Evidence: According to statistics, bomb builders are usually male.

Theory: The bomber probably worked at Con Edison in the past.
Evidence: He criticized Con Edison in his angry letters.

Theory: The bomber was paranoid. That's the strong feeling that someone is after you.
Evidence: The bomber believed that Con Edison was out to get him.

Theory: The bomber was about 50 years old.
Brussel's reasoning: Usually, **paranoia** peaks around age 35. The bomber planted his first bomb in 1940. If he were 35 then, he'd be about 50 in 1956.

Theory: The bomber was neat and skilled.
Evidence: He wrote his notes neatly. And the bombs were complex and carefully built.

Theory: The bomber had a high school education but did not go to college.

Evidence: He had probably learned the perfect handwriting in school. But his odd, stuffy language sounded self-taught.

Theory: The bomber was probably from Eastern or Central Europe.

Evidence: Protesters in Eastern and Central Europeans have a history of using bombs.

Theory: The bomber lived in Connecticut.

Evidence: Many Eastern and Central Europeans lived in Connecticut. Also, some of the letters had been mailed from a location between Connecticut and New York City.

Dr. Brussel had his profile, and he handed it over to the police. The bomber, he said, was a neat, middle-aged, paranoid Eastern European man from Connecticut.

Brussel went even further. The bomber, he said, would be dressed neatly. "When you catch him, he'll be wearing a double-breasted suit—and it will be buttoned."

Searching for a Madman
Police learn to use a profile.

Dr. Brussel told the police to release the profile to the media. He wanted the bomber to read about himself in the newspaper. The bomber enjoyed his game with the police. If the profile were wrong, he might brag about it in another letter. Eventually, he could get cocky and make a mistake.

The bomber soon proved Dr. Brussel right. After reading about the profile, he sent more letters to the media. He even called Dr. Brussel, but hung up quickly. In one of his letters, the bomber told about an accident he'd had at work. Detectives knew they were getting close.

Meanwhile, police gave the profile to Con Edison. A clerk searched their files for employees who fit the profile. Eventually, she found a file that looked promising. A man named George Metesky had been injured on the job. When he got sick with tuberculosis, he blamed it on the accident. He filed a claim for disability, asking Con Edison to pay him money. The company refused to pay.

Metesky then wrote angry letters to Con Edison. He mailed them from his home in

Waterbury, Connecticut. In one of the letters, he promised to take revenge for the company's "dastardly deeds."

The clerk handed over the file to her boss. Her boss passed it to police. They compared the details of the accident with the story the bomber told in his letter. They matched perfectly. Thanks to Dr. Brussel, detectives finally had their man.

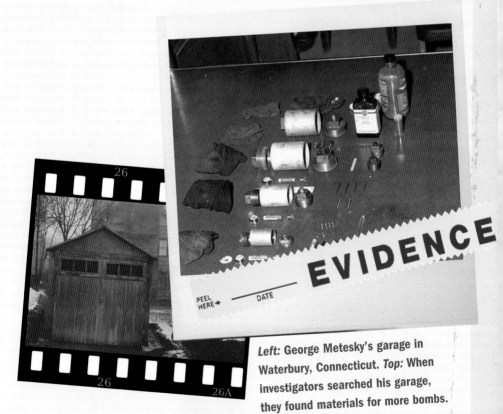

Left: George Metesky's garage in Waterbury, Connecticut. Top: When investigators searched his garage, they found materials for more bombs.

Caught!

Police arrest the Mad Bomber. He matches the profile perfectly—right down to the suit.

After his arrest, George Metesky posed for photographers. Underneath his overcoat, his double-breasted suit was neatly buttoned.

George Metesky lived in Waterbury with his two sisters. Neighbors described him as polite and neatly dressed. But he kept to himself. He went to New York City often. He attended Catholic mass. Beyond that, his neighbors knew little about him.

They were stunned when police came to Metesky's door. He greeted officers in his bathrobe. Right away, he confessed to being the bomber. He said that F.P. stood for "Fair Play."

Police allowed Metesky to change into street clothes. He put on a double-breasted suit—and it was buttoned!

At his trial, a jury found Metesky to be insane. The judge sent him to a mental hospital.

Dr. Brussel became famous. The New York City police often called him for help on important cases. His work helped give profilers a role in police departments around the world. After all, he described the Mad Bomber—right down to the clothes on his back. **24/7**

In this case, a profiler looked at several crimes to get a profile of the perp. What can a profiler do with only one crime? Find out in the next case.

The Case of the Too-Hot Fire

Firefighters discover a body inside a burning house, and a profiler takes the case.

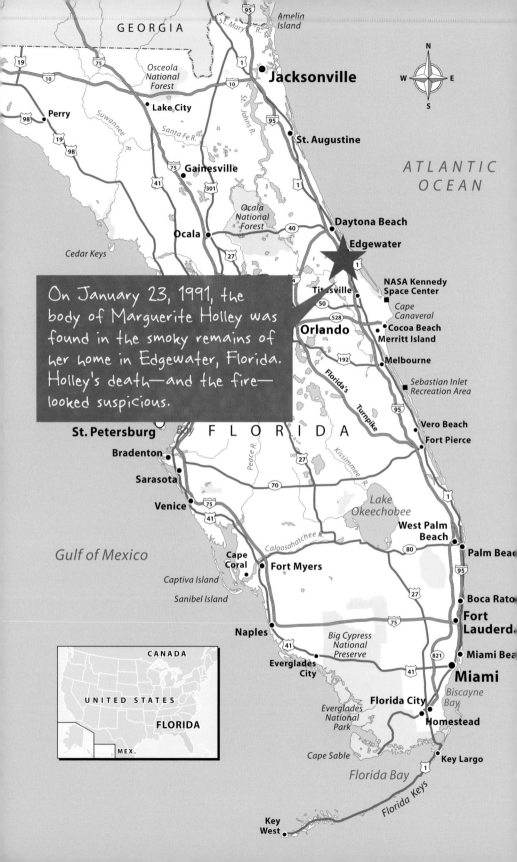

On January 23, 1991, the body of Marguerite Holley was found in the smoky remains of her home in Edgewater, Florida. Holley's death—and the fire—looked suspicious.

Fire!

A house goes up in flames—with a dead body inside.

At first it looked like a sad accident. Fire broke out in a house in Edgewater, Florida. It happened on the morning of January 23, 1991. Firefighters arrived on the scene and battled the flames. When they got the blaze under control, they entered the house. In the bedroom they found its owner, already dead on the floor.

The body belonged to Marguerite Holley, a grandmother and retired nurse. Next to her was a broken oil lamp. The fire had burned a hole in the floor.

At first glance, it seemed obvious what had happened. The oil lamp fell and set the floor on fire. The fire spread quickly and trapped Holley.

But as police looked around, a different story took shape. Holley's car was missing from the garage. Could it have been stolen? Glass had been broken out of a back-door window. Was that where the thief had entered the house?

Then there was the position of Holley's body. She lay flat on her back, arms at her sides. She didn't look like she had been fighting for her life. Finally, the hole in the floor

An oil lamp like this one was found next to the body of Marguerite Holley. Had it caused the fire in her house?

A fireman waits at Marguerite Holley's house for a police detective. The firemen had not known anyone was inside the house. They had put out the fire, discovered Holley's body, and then called the police.

seemed too big. Could an oil lamp have done that much damage?

Detectives sent Holley's body to the medical examiner for an **autopsy**. The autopsy should help answer the main question. Was Holley's death an accident, or murder?

Examining the Evidence

Was Marguerite Holley murdered?

When the **ME**'s report came in, detectives had their answer. The autopsy showed no soot or smoke in Holley's lungs. She hadn't breathed any smoke. She had been dead before the fire started. Holley had been strangled to death.

Police also ran lab tests on the bedroom floor. The tests found lighter fluid at the scene. That explained the damage to the floor. Someone had spread lighter fluid to start the fire.

Detectives now knew they were dealing with a homicide. But who would have reason to kill Marguerite Holley?

Police decided to bring in a criminal profiler.

The fire began here, in Holley's bedroom. Someone had used lighter fluid. That made the fire extremely hot. It also spread quickly and did a lot of damage.

The Profiler Steps In

Can Dayle Hinman figure out who might have killed Holley?

The Edgewater police called Dayle Hinman. Hinman often worked with Florida law enforcement on violent crime cases.

Hinman started with an important question: Was the killer a stranger? Or did Holley know her attacker?

After looking at crime scene photos, Hinman joined detectives at Holley's home.

The first thing she noted was the location of the house. It sat deep inside a quiet neighborhood, not on a main road.

Hinman then considered the timing of the murder. Holley died just before the fire started. The car had probably been taken right after the murder. That meant that the killer drove out of the neighborhood in broad daylight.

Dayle Hinman and another profiler, Wayne Porter, study a map that shows the area around Marguerite Holley's home.

Detectives showed Hinman the broken glass near the back door. The glass had fallen outside the door, not inside. The window had been broken from the inside.

After her investigation, Hinman decided that Holley had known her murderer.

How did she arrive at her conclusion? First, the house was far off the beaten path.

"It wasn't likely someone just happened to find her house," says Hinman. Second, the perp drove Holley's car through her neighborhood in broad daylight. He was probably someone who wouldn't look suspicious driving her car.

Hinman also reasoned that the killer had tried to cover his tracks. He probably broke the window to make the crime look like a robbery. And setting a fire in a home, Hinman says, is "almost always to try and cover up evidence."

WHO IS A PROFILER?
Profilers can be ...

Police detectives who do profiles as part of their criminal investigation.

Professors of criminology or psychologists. Law enforcement agencies call them to help out on cases.

FBI agents who have trained at the FBI's Behavioral Sciences Unit. They might profile international terrorists, as well as **serial** killers.

Agents at state investigative agencies who have training in behavioral science. For example, the Tennessee Bureau of Investigation has profilers.

Employees of large corporations or security firms. They might profile computer hackers or Internet criminals.

Police Close In

Hinman's conclusions help investigators focus on a suspect. Did the handyman do it?

Thanks to Hinman, the Edgewater detectives knew where to search for a suspect. They interviewed Holley's friends. Did anyone have a motive for killing Holley?

Their questions soon led to a handyman named John Smith. (That's not his real name.) Smith regularly did repair jobs around Holley's house. Friends said Holley thought Smith had been stealing from her.

Police tracked down people who knew Smith. Some of them claimed that he sometimes caused damage himself, then charged to repair it.

Investigators looked through Holley's records. Over the past six months, she had loaned Smith nearly $10,000.

The police got a warrant to search Smith's house. A police dog sniffed out a shirt in a pile of laundry. Tests later showed that the shirt contained lighter fluid. Investigators now had evidence to tie Smith to the fire.

Hinman's investigation pointed the police to the handyman, John Smith. This document shows the criminal profiling information on this suspect.

DC Number:	617886
Name:	
Race:	WHITE
Sex:	MALE
Hair Color:	BROWN
Eye Color:	HAZEL
Height:	5'06"
Weight:	178
Birth Date:	
Initial Receipt Date:	09/02/1992
Current Facility:	GLADES C. I.
Current Classification Status:	NOT APPLICABLE
Current Custody:	CLOSE
Current Release Date:	SENTENCED TO LIFE

Police arrested John Smith for the murder of Marguerite Holley. At his trial, the **prosecutor** described Smith's motive. He told the jury that Holley had grown tired of Smith's scams. Smith had killed her to prevent her from going to the police.

The jury believed the prosecutor. Smith was **convicted** and sentenced to life in prison.

The case left Hinman feeling satisfied with her work. "As a profiler, I look at a criminal's behavior for clues as to why he committed the crime," she says. "John Smith tried to hide his crime, and that's one of the things that led us to him." **24/7**

Investigators examine evidence at a crime scene. Hinman's examination of the crime scene helped her create a profile of the suspect in the Holley case.

In this case, a profiler helped find the perp by examining the physical evidence. But how will a profiler deal with digital evidence? Find out in the next case.

Montreal, Quebec, Canada
November 15, 1997
10:31 A.M.

The Case of the Mysterious Hacker

A university's computer network is under attack. Can a cyber-profiler find the hacker?

Note: The following case is true. Some places and names have been changed to protect people's privacy.

Making the Grade

A university's computer is hacked, and grades are changed. Is a student to blame?

Concordia University sits in the heart of Montreal, Quebec, in Canada. More than 30,000 students go to school there. Like most college students, they care about their grades.

Grades matter, and the university has a computer system that keeps track of them. Locked away in the computer network are the records for 30,000 people.

In November 1997, someone unlocked that system.

On the morning of November 15, a professor noticed something wrong. Student

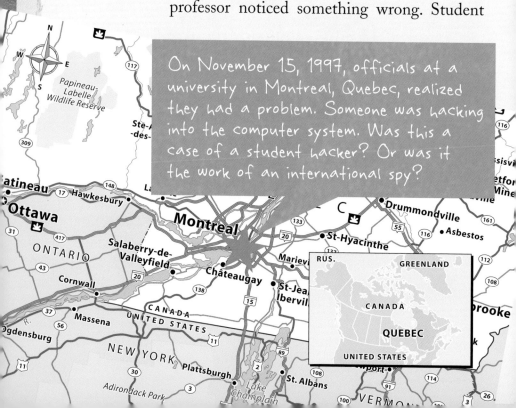

On November 15, 1997, officials at a university in Montreal, Quebec, realized they had a problem. Someone was hacking into the computer system. Was this a case of a student hacker? Or was it the work of an international spy?

grades in the computer files didn't match his records. He called the college's information technology (**IT**) staff. The IT staff logged into the system and found the problem. Someone was **hacking** into the system and changing grades.

The attack on the network wasn't just a prank. It was a crime under Canadian law. The college called the police. The police called computer **forensic** expert Dr. Marc Rogers.

The computer network at Concordia University has records on at least 30,000 people.

Nabbing an Amateur

Dr. Rogers follows the hacker's digital trail.

Dr. Rogers started with a basic question. Was the hacker a student who simply wanted better grades? Or was this the work of a professional with a bigger goal in mind?

Then he got to work collecting evidence. The crime scene, however, wasn't on any map. This criminal's trail began in **cyberspace**.

Rogers worked with the IT staff at the college. Together they figured out what Internet Service Provider (**ISP**) the hacker used.

Dr. Marc Rogers talks about cyber-profiling.

24/7: How is digital crime scene analysis different from psychological crime scene analysis?

DR. ROGERS: Our investigations parallel psychological crime scene analysis. What are the **signature** behaviors, **characteristics**, or MO of the criminal? How does that help you narrow down the suspect pool? And how do you get them to talk? When you push the right buttons, these guys love to talk. The longest statements I've ever taken are from computer criminals!

24/7: What kinds of cases do you work on?

DR. ROGERS: Basic hackers, Internet **predators**. We also deal with attacks on corporate computer systems. One of the first things we do is determine if the attacker was an insider or an outsider.

24/7: Are computer criminals different from regular criminals?

DR. ROGERS: [To computer criminals,] it seems like a faceless corporation they're going after, not a person. There's a layer of **technology** between them and their victims. These guys wouldn't rob a bank or attack someone. But they have no problem doing these things virtually.

Next, Dr. Rogers contacted the ISP. Normally, ISPs refuse to give out information about their users. But this user had broken the ISP's rules by hacking into the school's computer. Police in Montreal presented their case to a judge. The judge ordered the ISP to let Dr. Rogers onto their network.

Dr. Marc Rogers *(right)* often gives advice to people in law enforcement. Here, he's working with Dale Lloyd of the Indiana State Police.

Dr. Rogers drove to the offices of the ISP. He examined the **servers**. He followed the hacker's trail in computer records. The hacker had used well-known computer tools to unlock the university's system.

This was no skilled pro, Rogers decided. A professional would have written his own computer code. The hacker was most likely a student.

Dr. Rogers got the user's account information from the ISP. The police went to the hacker's home. The suspect was a student, and he confessed to hacking the university's system. He was expelled from school.

Case closed? Not quite.

A System Under Attack

The investigation goes further. Is there a professional hacker involved?

While Dr. Rogers was examining the ISP's servers, he discovered something suspicious. At certain times, the servers slowed down. After about an hour, they sped up again. Someone was running programs behind the server's normal activity.

This new activity didn't fit the MO of the student hacker. The programs were too complex. Someone else was at work here. At special times they logged in and took over the ISP. But why?

Was this hacker using the ISP to attack a larger computer system? If so, he could be a lot more dangerous than a student who wanted better grades.

Profile of a Pro

A second hacker is discovered—along with an international plot.

Dr. Rogers shifted his investigation to search for the new hacker.

At first, Rogers was confused by the system slowdowns. They happened regularly, always in the middle of the day. Rogers used his tracking software to trace the hacker.

The activity was coming from the former country of Yugoslavia. That explained the timing of the slowdowns. "The hacker was logging on in what was the middle of the night for him," says Dr. Rogers.

So the hacker worked in secret in the middle of the night. Why? What was the target? The answer was startling. The hacker was scanning the computers of the U.S. military.

Dr. Rogers now knew what he was dealing with. This was the work of a professional criminal or cyber-terrorist. It was time to hand the case over to the government.

CRIMINAL HACKERS

What kinds of people commit computer crimes?

Not all computer criminals are alike. But they do tend to fit a pattern. Here's Dr. Rogers's profile of a typical cyber-criminal.

- Most computer criminals are male.
- They aren't necessarily loners.
- They aren't necessarily smarter than other criminals.

- In general, computer criminals don't realize what they're doing is wrong. They don't always realize they're committing a crime.

The Feds Take Over

The discovery of a possible terrorist grabs the government's attention.

Dr. Rogers may have identified a major spying operation. He used plenty of high-tech tools to do it. But he still needed a profiler's basic skills.

Rogers understood the MOs of various types of hackers. That knowledge helped him tell the difference between a college student and an international hacker. Without it, the problem with the servers might have gone unexplained. Some might have thought it was the student hacker. Others would have looked for a technical problem.

Once Rogers had profiled the hacker, he was done with the case. Federal officials in Canada and the U.S. took over. It became a top-secret anti-terrorism investigation. Dr. Rogers never learned the outcome of the case. **24/7**

The country of Yugoslavia was formed in 1945. It started to break into different countries in the 1990s. Now, this area includes the countries of Bosnia and Herzegovina; Croatia; Montenegro; Republic of Macedonia; Serbia; and Slovenia.

FORENSIC DOWNLOAD

Here's your guide to the past, present, and future of criminal profiling.

IN THIS SECTION:

- ▶ how a BEHAVIOR PROFILE was created for Adolf Hitler;
- ▶ why CRIMINAL PROFILING is making headlines;
- ▶ tools profilers use to do their RESEARCH;
- ▶ whether criminal profiling might be in YOUR FUTURE.

1888 First Modern Criminal Profile

Someone is brutally murdering women in London. Police surgeon Dr. Thomas Bond performs an autopsy on the latest victim, Mary Kelly. Dr. Bond describes the kind of person who might have committed the murders. For example, he claims that the killer has some medical knowledge.

In the process, Dr. Bond creates the first modern "profile." His subject? One of history's most famous killers—Jack the Ripper! (This murderer may have written the letter to the left.)

Key Dates in Profiling

How did criminal profiling become a valuable part of police work?

Early 1940s Profiling at War

During World War II, German dictator Adolf Hitler is terrorizing the world. U.S. military leaders want to know more about him. They ask psychiatrist Walter Langer to create a profile of Hitler. Langer predicts that Hitler will kill himself rather than be captured. That prediction comes true.

1970 Setting Profiling Standards

FBI agent Howard Teten creates his first profile. Teten later develops the applied criminology course at the FBI National Academy. His work leads to the FBI's Behavioral Sciences Unit (BSU). The BSU trains profilers.

1978-83 Researching Serial Killers

FBI **agents** conduct a study of serial killers. They interview jailed murderers to see what they have in common. The researchers divide killers into two categories—organized and disorganized. This method is still used by some FBI profilers.

1981 Profiling Hits the Big Time

Thomas Harris publishes *Red Dragon*. The book introduces serial killer Hannibal Lecter. Harris follows *Red Dragon* with *The Silence of the Lambs* in 1988. The two books make the FBI's Behavioral Sciences Unit famous.

2002 Anthrax Attacker Stumps Profilers

Deadly anthrax spores are sent in the mail to public figures. FBI profilers decide that the attacks are the work of a single scientist. Four years later, the criminal has not been caught. The FBI profile is questioned. Some think the attacks were the work of terrorists.

2006 An Ever-Changing Field

Criminal profiling is growing and changing. As research on criminal activity grows, profilers get more scientific. They work with new techniques. Cyber-profilers, like Dr. Marc Rogers, use computer software to track criminals. So do geographic profilers. They use crime data to figure out where a criminal lives.

See Case #3: The Case of the Mysterious Hacker.

45

Real Profiler in the Spotlight

NEW YORK CITY—July 15, 2002

Broadcasting and Cable magazine reports that Court TV is adding a new reality show to their lineup. The show is called *Body of Evidence*. It will feature real-life profiler Dayle Hinman, one of the few women in the profession.

Hinman worked for 26 years in Florida's Department of Law Enforcement. She helped put hundreds of criminals behind bars. In *Body of Evidence*, Hinman re-creates the details of her most fascinating cases.

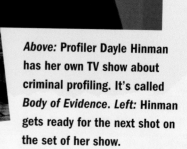

Above: Profiler Dayle Hinman has her own TV show about criminal profiling. It's called *Body of Evidence*. **Left:** Hinman gets ready for the next shot on the set of her show.

Ted Kaczynski had bombed universities and airlines since 1978. He was arrested in 1996. Here, he's being led to the courthouse in Helena, Montana, on April 4, 1996.

FBI Ignores Accurate Profile!

November 17, 1997

Bill Tafoya got it right. The FBI profiler tracked the Unabomber in 1993. The Unabomber had been sending bombs to universities and airlines since 1978.

Tafoya and fellow agent Mary Ellen O'Toole predicted that the bomber was in his early 50s. They thought he was well educated and hated technology.

The FBI ignored the profile. Instead, they looked for a younger man who worked in the airplane industry. They finally arrested Ted Kaczynski on April 3, 1996. He was 53, had a PhD, and hated technology.

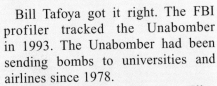

Kaczynski lived in this one-room cabin in Lincoln, Montana, for almost 25 years.

Body of Evidence

Have a look at the documents, tools, and software used by criminal profilers.

CRIME SCENE PHOTOS AND POLICE REPORTS

Many criminal profilers work from crime scene photos rather than going to the crime scene with the police. They can tell a lot from the position of a body, the wounds on a body, things left behind at a scene, how a victim was attacked, and so on.

[Forensic Fact]
Geographical profiling takes into account known movement patterns. For example, right-handed criminals escaping in a hurry flee to the left. They toss their weapons to the right. When lost, men tend to go downhill. Women tend to go uphill.

LAB REPORTS

Profilers must be able to read and understand lab reports by medical examiners, DNA specialists, and other forensic scientists. They gain important information from these reports, such as the cause of death and location of the wounds.

reports on insects found on corpse

FORENSIC ENTOMOLOGY DATA FORM

CASE NUMBER: _____

E: _____ AGENCY: _____

: Found: _____
I from Scene: _____

forest_____ field_____ pasture_____ brush_____ roadside_
barren area_____ closed building_____ open building_____
other_____
aburban: closed building_____ open building_____
vacant lot_____ pavement_____ trash container_____
other_____
habitat: pond_____ lake_____ creek_____ small river_____
large river_____ irrigation canal_____ ditch_____ gulf_____
swampy area_____ drainage ditch_____ salt water_____
fresh water_____ brackish water_____
other_____
e: Open air_____ burial/depth_____
clothing entire_____ partial_____ nude_____
portion of body clothed_____
description of clothing _____
type of debris on body_____
decomposition: fresh_____ bloat_____ active decay_____
advanced decay_____ skeletonization_____ saponification_
mummification_____ dismemberment_____
other: _____
ngers: _____
c injury sites: (Comment or draw below)

;: ambient:_____ ambient (1ft) _____ body surface_____
und surface_____ under-body interface_____ maggot mass____
ter temp. if aquatic_____ enclosed structure_____ AC/Heat- o
ling fan- on/off_____ soil temperature- 10cm_____ 20cm___
d samples _____ Number of live samples _____
emperatures periodically each day at the site for 3-5 days after bod
COPYRIGHT DR. J. H. BYRD ©1998-2000

CAPMI SYMBOLS

PRIMARY CODES		SECONDARY CODES	
C	CROWN	A	ANOMALY, ROOT TIP, ANY PATHOLOGY
D	DISTAL	B	PRIMARY TOOTH
F	FACIAL	G	GOLD, CAST METAL
L	LINGUAL		STAINLESS STEEL
M	MESIAL	N	NON-METALLIC
O	OCCLUSAL/INCISAL		RESTORATION
U	UNERUPTED	P	PONTIC
V	VIRGIN TOOTH	R	ROOT CANAL FILLING
X	MISSING TOOTH	S	SILVER AMALGAM
I	JAW FRAGMENT	T	REMOVABLE PROS
	MISSING,	Z	CARIES
	NONRECOGNIZABLE,		
	FRACTURED CROWN,		
	TRAUMATIC AVULSION		

X-Ray Type: _____ Date: _____
X-Ray Type: _____ Date: _____
X-Ray Type: _____ Date: _____
Examiners: _____

ANOMALY, ROOT TIP,
ANY PATHOLOGY
PRIMARY TOOTH
OLD, CAST METAL,
AINLESS STEEL
N-METALLIC
STORATION
NTIC
T CANAL FILLING
ER AMALGAM
OVABLE PROS
ES

forensic dental forms

ay Type: _____ Date: _____
X-Ray Type: _____ Date: _____
Examiners: _____ Date: _____

REMARKS

RESEARCH

Profilers also read books, articles, and research by psychologists and other profilers. They might compare cases they're working on to similar cases that have been solved by other profilers. They keep up-to-date on the latest psychological research and developments in forensic science.

Profilers may also use these tools.

geographical profiling software: used to map locations of crimes to predict where the perp lives.

cyber-profiling software: used to track down the location of the computer used by a hacker or an Internet predator.

VICAP: a database with information about violent crimes, especially murder. VICAP stands for *Violent Criminal Apprehension Program*.

CODIS: the FBI's DNA database. It contains DNA samples of more than 300,000 convicted criminals. CODIS stands for *Combined DNA Index System*.

AFIS: That's a computer database where police can store the prints of arrested suspects. AFIS stands for *Automated Fingerprint Identification System*.

NETWORKING

Profilers often work with other profilers, psychologists, and police **experts**. Many develop ongoing relationships with these professionals and ask their opinions on cases.

"I'm part of a group of 150 forensic scientists who use a secure Web site to share information," says profiler Dayle Hinman. "These are profilers, psychologists, and medical examiners from all over the world.

"If I want the opinion of other profilers, I can go to this Web site. I can give the group information on a case. They can tell me what they think. I may not have all the answers, but I know who to ask!"

HELP WANTED:
Criminal Profiler

Are you interested in investigating criminal profiling? Here's more information about the field.

Q&A: DAYLE HINMAN
DR. MARC ROGERS
DR. MAURICE GODWIN

Criminal profiler Dayle Hinman is the star of the Court TV series *Body of Evidence: From the Case Files of Dayle Hinman.*

24/7: How did you get into this field?

ROGERS: I had a degree in criminology and psychology, and then I became a law enforcement officer. I was working on my PhD in forensic psychology. I became interested in understanding why people commit criminal acts using technology. So all my interests seemed to meld together.

HINMAN: I was career law enforcement. I received a fellowship at the FBI's Behavioral Science Unit. I wanted to be the person out there trying to find out what happened and why. [I didn't want to be] the secretary who typed the report about it!

51

24/7: What do you like about your job?

HINMAN: I like everything about it. You would expect that my job would be depressing, but it's not. You do have to deal with a lot of people who are dead or dying. But I like being able to focus an investigation on the type of person who committed a crime. I like being part of the team that figures out who did it.
GODWIN: A lot of what I like is the mystery. It appeals to my curiosity. It's a challenge to find out who did it.

24/7: What skills come in handy for a profiler?

GODWIN: The first thing you need is curiosity—to search and find the unknown. You also need logic. They even teach logic courses at universities.

HINMAN: I see the ability to observe and the ability to listen as important attributes. So few people go to a crime scene and actually see what's there. You have to notice all the details. And you need to be someone who takes the job seriously and works hard.

Cyber-profiler Dr. Marc Rogers is a professor of cyber-forensics at Purdue University in Indiana.

24/7: What advice do you have for young people interested in this field?

GODWIN: You must have a solid background in psychology. And for geographical profiling, statistics courses are good. It also helps to have courses in criminal investigation and forensic science. And once you get your degree, join professional organizations and go to conferences and such. Most profilers are **consultants**, so it's good to get your name out there.

THE STATS

DAY JOB
Many criminal profilers are practicing psychologists. Others are specially trained police officers. Still others are FBI agents. Even professors of criminology are called on to consult when they're needed.

MONEY
Police officers average between $34,000 and $56,000 a year. Psychologists average between $41,000 and $65,000 a year. FBI agents start at $48,000 a year.

EDUCATION
Criminal profilers must finish four years of college. FBI agents must finish four years of college and train to become an FBI agent. They must join the FBI's Behavioral Sciences Unit.

HINMAN: I think it helps to have law enforcement experience.

ROGERS: I'm starting to see lots more students in this field.

Young people are not as freaked out by technology as the older behavioral scientists might have been. I think if you're interested in computers and criminology, this is a growing field for you.

Dr. Maurice Godwin develops psychological profiles of criminals. He also creates geographical profiles to show where suspects probably live.

53

DO YOU HAVE WHAT IT TAKES?

Take this totally unscientific quiz to find out if criminal profiling might be a good career for you.

1 **Do you have good instincts about people?**
   a) Yes, I can usually tell what someone is like.
   b) Sometimes, but I've made some major mistakes.
   c) I like everyone, so I often am disappointed in people.

2 **Are you curious and logical?**
   a) Yes, I'm always asking questions and I come up with pretty good conclusions.
   b) I'm a little curious about some things.
   c) Not really. I tend to look at situations and jump to conclusions.

3 **Would you say you work well with others?**
   a) Yes, I'm most creative when I'm part of a group.
   b) Most of the time.
   c) I'm a loner. People often get on my nerves!

4 **How do you think you respond to news about violent and disturbing crimes?**
   a) It upsets me, but I mostly just hope the perp is caught.
   b) Sometimes I really just can't listen.
   c) Don't tell me about that kind of stuff. I can't take it!

5 **Do you enjoy studying behavior and understanding why people do what they do?**
   a) Yes, that's so cool.
   b) Sometimes.
   c) No, that's pretty boring.

YOUR SCORE
Give yourself 3 points for every "a" you chose. Give yourself 2 points for every "b" you chose. Give yourself 1 point for every "c" you chose.

If you got **13–15 points**, you'd probably be a good criminal profiler.
If you got **10–12 points**, you might be a good criminal profiler.
If you got **5–9 points**, you might want to look at another career!

2 3 4 5 6 7 8 9 10

HOW TO GET STARTED...NOW!

It's never too early to start working toward your goals.

GET AN EDUCATION

▶ Focus on behavior science classes (like psychology or sociology) and computer science.

▶ Start thinking about college. Look for ones with good forensic science or computer forensic programs.

▶ Read the newspaper. Keep up with what's going on in your community.

▶ Read anything you can find about criminal profiling and psychology.

▶ See the books and Web sites in the Resources section on pages 56–58.

▶ Graduate from high school!

NETWORK!

Find out about forensic groups in your area. See if you can find a local criminal profiler who might be willing to give you advice.

GET AN INTERNSHIP

Look for an internship with a local law enforcement agency. Look for an internship at a local medical examiner's office.

LEARN ABOUT OTHER JOBS IN THE FIELD

Employees of large corporations or security firms sometimes profile hackers or Internet criminals.

Resources

Looking for more information about criminal profiling? Here are some resources you don't want to miss!

PROFESSIONAL ORGANIZATIONS

Academy of Behavioral Profiling (ABP)
www.profiling.org/abp_about.html
Academy of Behavioral Profiling
336 Lincoln Street, P.O. Box 6406
Sitka, AK 99835
PHONE: 831-254-5446

The ABP is a professional organization that promotes education and training for criminal profilers.

American Academy of Forensic Sciences (AAFS)
www.aafs.org
410 North 21st Street
Colorado Springs, CO 80904-2798
PHONE: 719-636-1100

The AAFS is an organization for forensic scientists. It helps them meet and share information with other forensic experts. The AAFS sponsors seminars and conferences. Its Web site includes a long list of colleges and universities with forensic science programs.

Canadian Society of Forensic Science (CSFS)
www.csfs.ca
P.O. Box 37040
3332 McCarthy Road
Ottawa, Ontario
Canada K1V 0W0
PHONE: 613-738-0001
E-MAIL: csfs@bellnet.ca

This nonprofit organization promotes the study of forensic science. Its Web site has information about careers and schools with forensic programs.

EDUCATION AND TRAINING

The AAFS Web site **(www.aafs.org)** has a list of colleges and universities with forensic science programs.

Federal Bureau of Investigation (FBI)
www.fbi.gov/
J. Edgar Hoover Building
935 Pennsylvania Avenue, NW
Washington, DC 20535-0001
PHONE: 210-567-3177
E-MAIL: smile@uthscsa.edu

The FBI Web site contains information on its latent print unit. Its Behavioral Science Unit also gives information on getting a job with the FBI (click on "training").

Royal Canadian Mounted Police (RCMP)
**www.rcmp-grc.gc.ca/
techops/recruiting_e.htm**
RCMP Headquarters
1200 Vanier Parkway
Ottawa, Ontario
Canada K1A 0R2
PHONE: 613-993-7267

The RCMP is the Canadian national police service. Its Web site gives information on different jobs within the RCMP, including the investigative behavioral sciences programs.

WEB SITES

Center for Investigative Psychology
www.i-psy.com/
This Web site gives information about conferences and provides links to recent published studies in the field.

Court TV's Crime Library
www.crimelibrary.com
For a variety of information about forensic science.

Environmental Criminology Research, Inc.
www.ecricanada.com/
The Web site for this company contains information on geographic profiling.

Forensic Solutions, LLC
www.corpus-delicti.com/
The Web site for this company contains information on profiling, suggested reading, and a list of helpful resources.

BOOKS

Camenson, Blythe. *Opportunities in Forensic Science Careers.* New York; McGraw-Hill, 2001.
This book has information about training, education, salaries, and career opportunities in the field of forensic science.

Campbell, Andrea. *Crime Scene (Detective Notebook).* New York: Sterling, 2004.
Kids will learn about what it really takes to bring criminals to justice: what good evidence is, how to use memory and observation, and what an important role science plays.

Dahl, Michael. *Computer Evidence (Forensic Crime Solvers).* Kentwood, La.: Edge Books, 2004. This book looks at solving crimes in cyberspace.

Donkin, Andrew. *Crime Busters.* New York: DK Publishing, 2001.
Kids will learn how law enforcement masterminds catch the criminals.

Esherick, Joan. *Criminal Psychology and Personality Profiling.* Broomall, Pa.: Mason Crest Publishers, 2005.
This book explains how profilers come up with their suspects.

Fisher, Barry A. J. *Techniques of Crime Scene Investigation, 7th ed.* Boca Raton, Fla.: CRC Press, 2003. This is an introduction to the techniques real crime scene investigators use.

Genge, Ngaire, E. *The Forensic Casebook: The Science of Crime Scene Investigation.* New York: Ballantine, 2002.
This book looks at all kinds of forensic crime-fighting. It also has information on jobs and training programs.

Platt, Richard. *Crime Scene: Ultimate Guide to Forensic Science.* New York: DK Publishing, 2006.
This book takes a look at the latest high-tech tools being used in forensic science.

Rainis, Kenneth G. *Crime-Solving Science Projects: Forensic Science Experiments.* Berkeley Heights, N.J.: Enslow Publishing, 2000.
Students learn about fingerprints, fibers, blood evidence, and other factors of forensic science.

Walker, Pam, and Elaine Wood. *Crime Scene Investigations: Real-Life Science Labs for Grades 6–12.* New York: Jossey-Bass, 1998.
Find step-by-step experiments so kids can solve crimes just like real forensic scientists.

A

AFIS (AY-fis) *noun* a computer database in which police store the prints of arrested suspects. AFIS stands for *Automated Fingerprint Identification System*.

agent (AY-juhnt) *noun* a person trained to do a job for a company or government organization

autopsy (AH-top-see) *noun* a medical exam done on a dead body to figure out the cause of death

B

behavior (bih-HAYV-yer) *noun* the way a person acts or responds to certain conditions. Behavioral sciences are sciences that study the ways people behave.

C

characteristics (ka-rik-tuh-RISS-tiks) *noun* qualities, features, or marks that help identify something

CODIS (KOH-diss) *noun* a database that contains DNA samples of more than 300,000 people. It stands for *Combined DNA Index System*.

consultant (kun-SUL-tant) *noun* an expert who charges a fee to provide advice or services in a particular field

convict (con-VIKT) *verb* to find guilty in a court of law

criminal profiling (KRIM-uh-nul PRO-file-ing) *noun* the process of using evidence from a crime scene and knowledge of psychology to predict a criminal's characteristics and personality. Also known as "psychological crime scene analysis."

criminology (KRIM-un-OL-uh-gee) *noun* the scientific study of crime, criminals, criminal behavior, and corrections. A criminologist is an expert in criminology.

cyberspace (SYE-bur-spayss) *noun* the whole communications universe available on a computer. The prefix *cyber-* refers to that computer world.

D

dastardly (DAS-tard-lee) *adjective* being cowardly and dishonest

database (DAY-tuh-bayss) *noun* a lot of information organized on a computer

device (di-VYSSE) *noun* a piece of equipment for a certain job

DNA (DEE-en-ay) *noun* a chemical found in almost every cell of your body. It's a blueprint for the way you look and function.

E

evidence (EHV-uh-denss) *noun* materials, facts, and details collected from a crime scene that may be clues about the crime

expert (EX-purt) *noun* a person who has a great deal of knowledge and experience about something. See page 12 for a list of forensic experts.

F

FBI (ef-BEE-eye) *noun* a U.S. government agency that investigates major crimes. It's short for *Federal Bureau of Investigation*.

forensic (fur-REN-zik) *adjective* describing the science used to investigate and solve crimes

H

hack (hak) *verb* to illegally break into a computer system; a person who does this is a hacker

homicide (HOM-uh-side) *noun* a common law enforcement term for murder

I

ID (EYE-dee) *noun* the process of figuring out who someone is. It's short for *identification*.

ISP (EYE-ess-pee) *noun* a company that supplies Internet service. It's short for *Internet service provider*.

IT (eye-TEE) *noun* a department that helps keep computers running smoothly. It's short for *information technology*.

M

ME (EM-ee) *noun* a person who works in a crime lab and studies bodies. An ME figures out how and when a person died, and what kinds of weapons made the wounds. It's short for *medical examiner*.

MO (EM-oh) *noun* it's short for *modus operandi*, which means "method of operation." It's how a criminal operates.

motive (MOH-tiv) *noun* the reason for doing something. Criminal profilers look for the perp's motive for committing the crime.

P

paranoia (PAIR-ah-noy-uh) *noun* a disorder in which someone becomes extremely suspicious of everyone else

perp (purp) *noun* a common law enforcement term for a person who commits a crime. It's short for the word *perpetrator*.

predator (PRED-uh-tur) *noun* someone who tries to hurt others

professor (pruh-FESS-ur) *noun* a teacher at a college or university

prosecutor (PROSS-uh-kyoo-tur) *noun* a lawyer who represents the government in criminal trials

psychology (sye-KOL-uh-gee) *noun* the scientific study of the human mind and human behavior

S

serial (SEER-ee-ul) *adjective* done repeatedly or in a series

server (SUR-vur) *noun* a computer in a network that helps the other computers run

signature (SIG-nuh-chur) *noun* a characteristic mark

staging (STAY-jing) *noun* the way items are arranged or placed at a crime scene

stats (stats) *noun* official numbers about events that have happened in the past. It's short for *statistics*.

suspect (SUHS-pekt) *noun* a person law enforcement officials think might be guilty of a crime

T

technology (tek-NOL-uh-jee) *noun* the development of new machines, devices, or techniques

theory (THEE-ur-ee) *noun* an idea that explains how something could have happened

V

VICAP (VYE-kap) *noun* a database that contains lots of information about terrible crimes. It's short for *Violent Criminal Apprehension Program*.

victimology (vik-tim-AH-luh-jee) *noun* the study of how people become victims, or targets of crimes

Index

Author's Note

Like a lot of people, I was a big fan of the criminal profilers I saw on TV and in the movies.

Hollywood always seems to play up the "gut instincts" of the investigators, making profilers seem like psychics who know what the killer is thinking. I now know just how much science is behind real criminal profiling.

If you want to learn more about psychological crime scene analysis, follow the trail I took: Start with the Web sites listed in the Resources section. If you like reading about cases, try the Court TV site.

The sites for professional organizations give info on getting a job in the field. And you can always type "criminal profiling" into the search engine on your computer and get lots of interesting links.

You can also read news articles about famous profiling cases, or check out books by well-known profilers. You can even find profiling textbooks at bookstores, but they can be pretty complicated, so have your dictionary handy!

The big surprise in my research was how much the profiling field is changing and how much controversy surrounds it. There are several teaching methods, each involving a different type of science and research. The field is a lot more complicated than it seems!

I have to say, as cool as the job looks, I could never be a profiler. Just reading all the murder cases made me double-lock my doors!

ACKNOWLEDGMENTS

I would like to thank the following people and organizations for their time and cooperation. I couldn't have written this book without their help.

Dayle Hinman
Dr. Maurice Godwin
Dr. Marc Rogers
Dr. Robert Keppel
Court TV
American Academy of Forensic Sciences

CONTENT ADVISERS:
H.W. "Rus" Ruslander, Forensic Supervisor, Palm Beach County (Florida) Medical Examiner's Office
Donna Brandelli, MFS, Forensic Identification Specialist